Life

Live

Life Live
February 24 - April 14, 2018

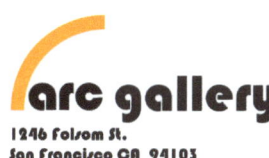

arc gallery
1246 Folsom St.
San Francisco CA 94103

Curator's Statement

The 8th Annual "Life Live" assembles five amazing practitioners of life drawing. Arc Fine Arts Consulting will be exhibiting their work in the Project Gallery. On Saturday, March 10th, the artists will be showcasing their skills "live" in figure drawing sessions open to the public in the main gallery. The gestural drawings will be ripped from their sketchbooks & displayed where they will be immediately for sale at $100 each.

Arc Fine Arts Consulting is established as a natural extension of the mission of Arc Gallery and Studios. Arc is dedicated to showcasing and promoting emerging and established artists in the San Francisco Bay Area. Here we are blessed with some of the most prestigious art schools in the country. On a per capita basis San Francisco boasts a higher percentage of working artists than any other city in the country. The opportunity for local collectors and businesses to build collections which tap into and support these communities is unparalleled. Arc Fine Arts is singularly dedicated to fostering those connections.

Curator:

Michael Yochum a co-founder of Arc Gallery & Studios, along with Matthew Frederick, Stephen C. Wagner and Priscilla Otani.

Catalog designed by Michael Yochum
Arc Gallery © 2018

Featured Artists

Arlene Diehl
Susan R. Kirshenbaum
Gail Ragains
Eric Saint Georges
Julianne Wallace Sterling

OPENING RECEPTION
Saturday, February 24th, 7-9 PM

LIFE LIVE Live Drawing Event
Saturday, March 10th, 6:30-10 PM

CLOSING RECEPTION
Saturday, April 14th, 12-3 PM

Arlene Diehl

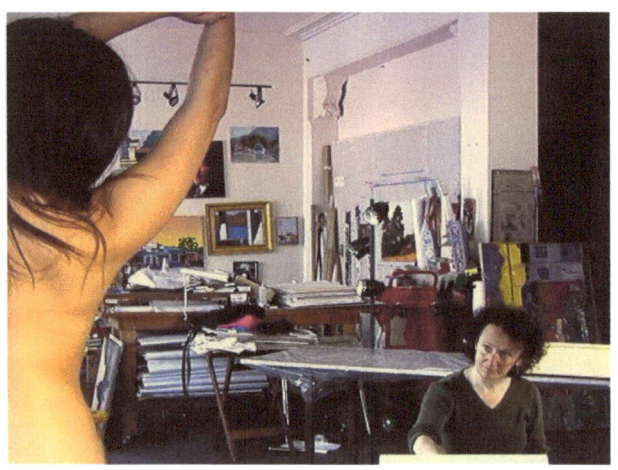

My work has evolved from a lifelong love for, fascination with, and sense of reverence for the human form. I have also been deeply committed over the years to the process of drawing, finding in it time and again an emotional and visceral immediacy that has served my deeper purposes. I am working now exclusively with live models and with a great deal of speed. I like working with a living, breathing human being because, by definition, the subject is not a static one but a dynamic one, moment by moment in a process of change. My aim is to transmit something of the power of that dynamism to the viewer.

This process requires of me a very deep letting off of the brakes of any preconceived notions I may have had for the drawing. By responding freshly to a particular moment the work can move in many different directions, sometimes more abstractly, sometimes more representationally. My best work often includes elements of both, and can be further layered with a sense of transition, emotional nuance and some measure of mystery.

website: https://www.artspan.org/artist/artistsartist
email: adiehl@sonic.net

ARLENE DIEHL was born in Massachusetts and raised in New England. Since 1990, she has lived here in San Francisco. She has exhibited her work continuously since her adolescence, in Boston, on Cape Cod, in the Bay Area, Los Angeles, Palm Desert, Australia and had her first solo show in Europe (July 2013); in the Netherlands.

EARLY RECOGNITION:

At 16, Arlene received the prestigious Strathmore Award in Drawing awarded annually to one high school student nationwide. (Exhibition/Competition N.Y. NY 1973) At 17, her self-portrait appeared on the cover of Senior Scholastic Magazine, her work was favorably noted in New York Magazine and she received a Merit Scholarship to Boston University School for the Arts(1974). She later transferred to the Boston Museum of Fine Arts School.(75-79)

SELECT SOLO EXHIBITIONS:

2013	*Mensielijk Lichaam (Human Bodies,* Gallery 0-68, Velp, The Netherlands
2012	*Drawings: Arlene Diehl,* Emac & Lawton PTY LTD, Botany, Australia
2006	*Figuration: Nineteen Drawings and One Bronze,* Anderson Smith North, San Rafael, CA
2004	*XY-zy: The Male Nude,* Klein's Exhibition Space, San Francisco, CA
2002	*Recent Drawings,* Reverie Gallery Cafe, San Francisco, CA
	Speaking Figuratively, Klein's Exhibition Space, San Francisco, CA

SELECT GROUP EXHIBITIONS:

2011-17	*Life Live I - VIII,* exhibition and live life drawing, Arc Gallery, San Francisco CA
2015	*The LGBT Show,* Linus Gallery, Los Angeles CA
2013	*Art Auction XV,* curated exhibition, Long Beach Museum of Art, Long Beach CA
2011	*The Figure Now,* Fontbonne University Fine Arts Gallery, St. Louis MO
2010	*Blake Collects: Living With Art,* Martha Bennett Gallery, Minneapolis MN
2008	*Articulating Art,* Left Coast Galleries, Studio City CA
	One Night Stand: Nude, Sensual and Erotic Work, ARTworkSF Gallery, San Francisco CA
2006	*Gestures In And On Paper: Original Works by Arlene Diehl, David Einstein and Minjung Kim,* Modern Masters Fine Art , Palm Desert, CA

COMMISSIONS: Arlene was commissioned to do a large (5 ft by 6 ½ ft.) charcoal drawing of ballroom dancers, interpreted from a 1950's Henri Cartier-Bresson photograph (1999) and also more recently to do a series of charcoal nudes of writer and poet Jewelle Gomez.

COMMUNITY::   Arlene is on the Board of Directors (and former acting president) of Red Umbrellas, a juried non-profit artists' exhibition group based in San Francisco.

PUBLICATIONS: Cover art: "Godin, held" by novelist Gustaf Peek (published in Dutch, 2014) Original drawings for "Tussen Malaise en Magie; Theater in het leven, Leven in het theater" 2011 Thomas de Neve (published in Dutch and German, 2012)

REPRESENTATION: Arlene is being represented by Art Gallery 0-68, in Velp, The Netherlands, Left Coast Galleries Studio City, CA., Rachelle Ryan Gallery Portland. OR, and by Emac & Lawton PTY LTD, Botany, AU

COLLECTIONS: Arlene's work is included in private collections across the United States and Canada, as well as in Great Britain, France, Germany, Ireland, Italy, Austria, The Netherlands, Hungary, New Zealand, Australia, Taiwan, Malaysia, The Philippines, Mexico, Honduras and Brazil.

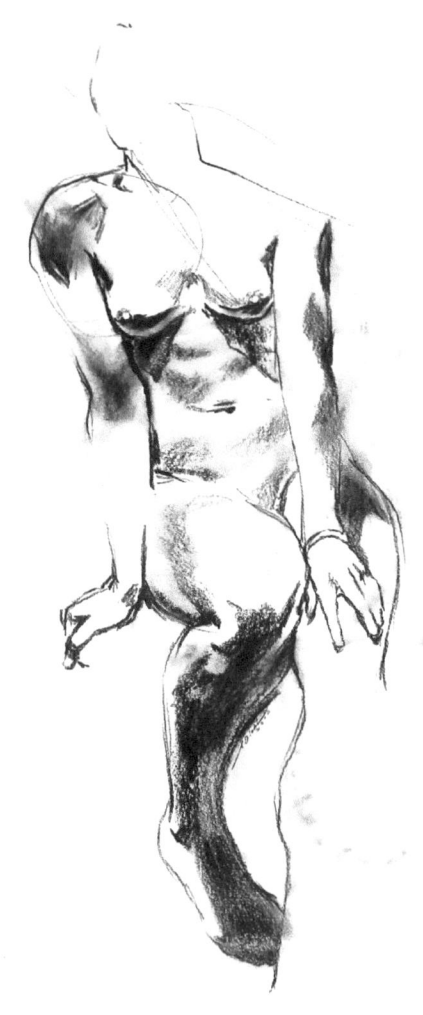

Untitled Two
compressed charcoal on paper
22" x 38" $1050

Arlene Diehl

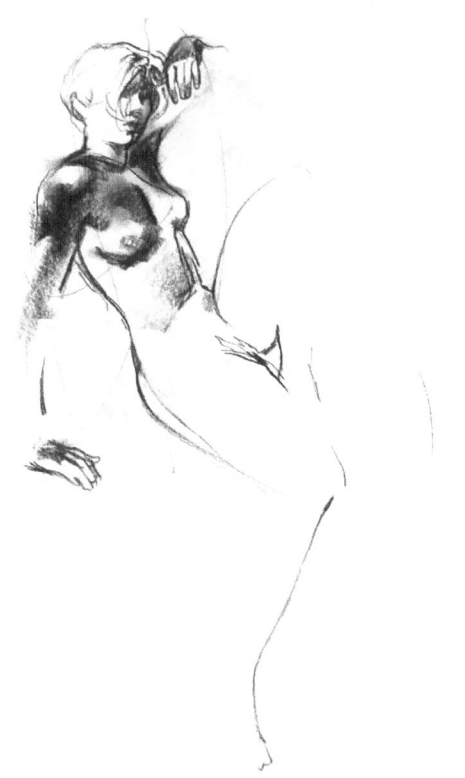

Untitled One
compressed charcoal on paper
22" x 37" $950

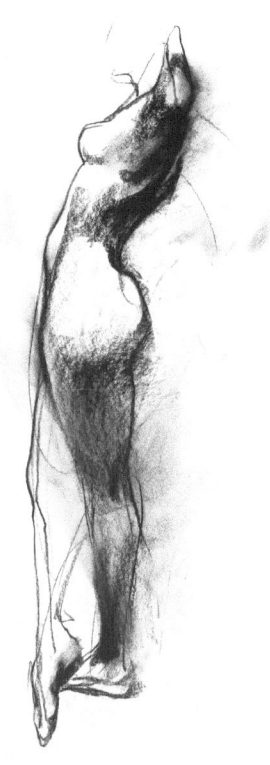

Untitled Three
compressed charcoal on paper
20" x 37" $950

Arlene Diehl

Susan R. Kirshenbaum

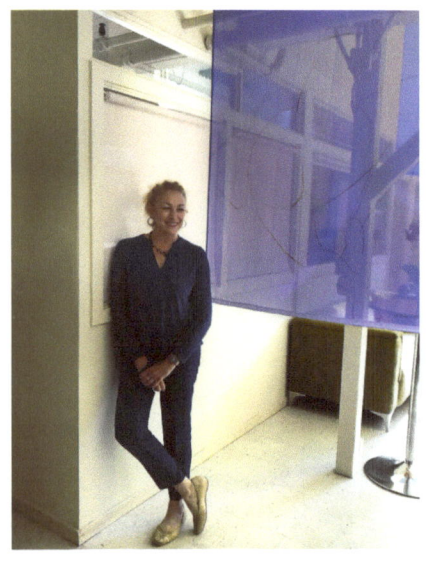

"My family was unconventional and proud of it. These are powerful forces that make me who I am. Art is one way for me to express my activism."

My subjects are naked but are completely comfortable in their skins. Are you? Do you want to be? Nudity is not an issue. Body love is. My drawings and paintings convey frankness and feel intimate and natural. These are real people who come across as strong, decisive, confident, and unique individuals – this is my underlying narrative.

Drawn from live, nude models, they are gestural, graphic, sensual, and fluid. Frequently combined with my photos and paintings, my life drawings take on universal meanings and narratives. I have always been focused on people, reflecting a desire to convey our everyday humanity and motivates people to embrace their human-ness and imperfections. I identify with my models and they become our shared story. It's fundamental to me to show who we are and to fight to remain uncensored. My work is feminist and confrontational, yet rich color, line, texture, and composition are of equally importance. Working digitally with my iPad Pro and Apple Pencil helps me work fast, see my process, and test possibilities.

website: http://www.cherrypits.net/
email: srkirshenbaum@gmail.com

SUSAN R. KIRSHENBAUM is a San Francisco-based figurative artist with a life-long commitment to art making. She grew up in a family of visual artists who founded and ran the Ivy School of Professional Art in Pittsburgh, PA, where she studied and worked from age 5 to 25.

Since Ivy, she's taken courses at SFAI, CCA, UC Berkeley Extension, Kala, City College, and in Girona, Spain. In 2016 Kirshenbaum returned to full-time art making after a long career as a creative director for marketing and branding.

Kirshenbaum has exhibited in group and solo shows in Pittsburgh, and the San Francisco Bay Area. Her works are in collections nationally and internationally. Living and working in San Francisco, California since 1980, she's taken breaks to live in Hawaii, NYC, and Spain. She can be found making art at her hilltop home with her cats and husband nearby.

SELECT SOLO EXHIBITIONS:

2018	*Reveals*, Secret Agent, San Francisco, CA
2017	*Exposed*, Bayview Boat Club, San Francisco, CA
	Figuratively Speaking, The Troll House, San Francisco, CA
	And Figuratively Speaking, site-specific installation, The Troll House, San Francisco, CA
2016	*Susan R. Kirshenbaum*, The Laundry, San Francisco, CA

SELECT JURIED GROUP EXHIBITIONS:

2018	*Snap!*, Arc Gallery, San Francisco, CA
	Eye of the Beholder, SFWA, San Francisco, CA
	Discover, SFWA, San Francisco, CA
	Paradise Lost, Invitational Figurative Group Show, Back to the Picture, San Francisco, CA
2017	*Reflection*, SFWA, San Francisco, CA
	Members Show, Art Guild of Pacifica, Pacifica, CA (Merit Award Winner)
	Loving Golden Gate Park, SFWA, San Francisco, CA
	New Works, SFWA, San Francisco, CA
	mDAC Summit (Mobile Art), Pacific Art League, Palo Alto, CA
	Science, Tech and Art, Pacific Art League, Palo Alto, CA
	City, Sea, Landscape, SFWA, San Francisco, CA
	All Botanical, SFWA, San Francisco, CA
	Summer Exposure, Pacific Art League, Palo Alto, CA
	ArtSpan Group Exhibition, stARTup Art Fair, San Francisco, CA

ART RESIDENCIES:

2017	The Troll House, Co-work space and Gallery, Pier 26, San Francisco, CA
2016	The Laundry, Mission District, San Francisco, CA

RELATED VOLUNTEER WORK:

2007-10	Board of Directors: River of Words – an educational nonprofit for children's art and poetry, co-founders: Poet Laureate Robert Hass and Pam Michael
1993-94	Planning Committee and Participant: City of Poets with Annice Jacoby and Lisa Citron | The Roof is on Fire with Suzanne Lacey, Annice Jacoby, and Chris Johnson

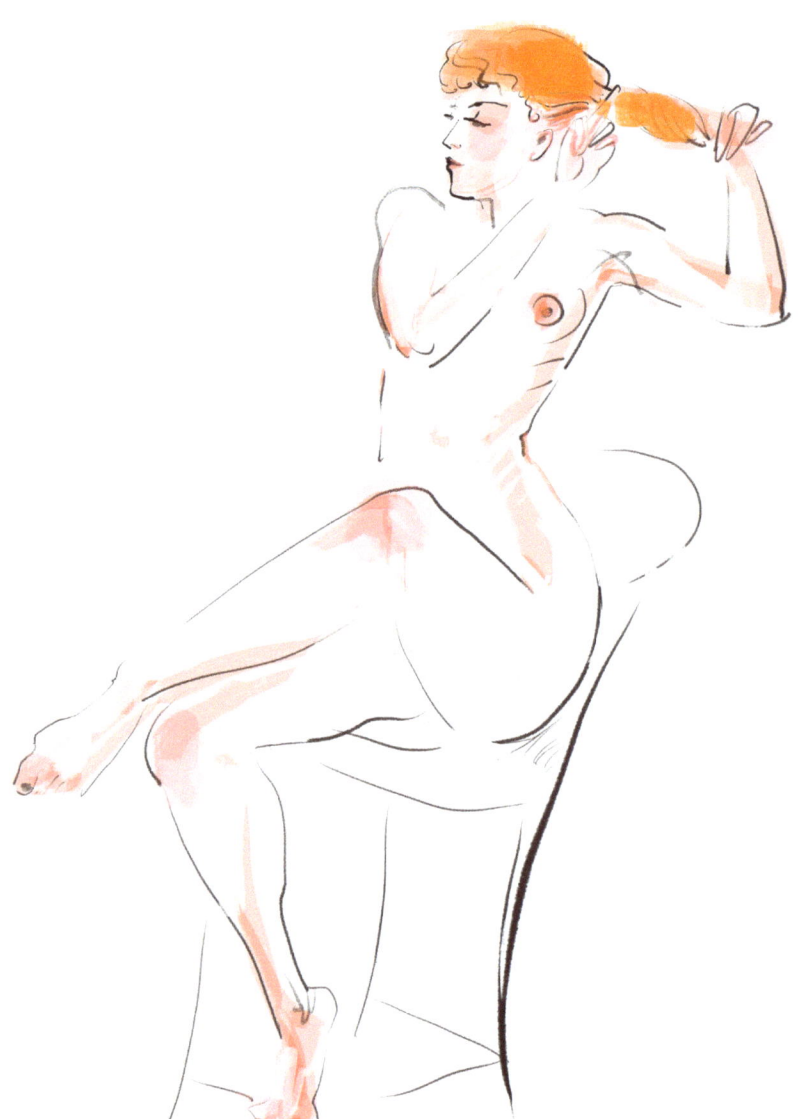

Red Hair, Curly and Straight (White Scroll Series)
mixed media - created on iPad, printed on silk
46" x 72"
$1800
(limited edition 1/3, hand signed & numbered)

Susan R. Kirshenbaum

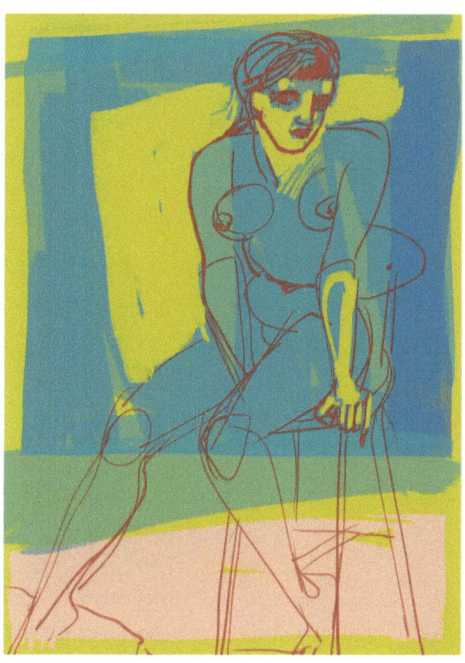

Listening to You (Abstracts Series)
mixed media collage - created on iPad, fine art print
19" x 25"
$625
(limited edition 1/1, hand signed & numbered)

Protected (Abstracts Series)
mixed media collage - created on iPad, fine art print
20" x 26"
$625
(limited edition AP, hand signed & numbered)

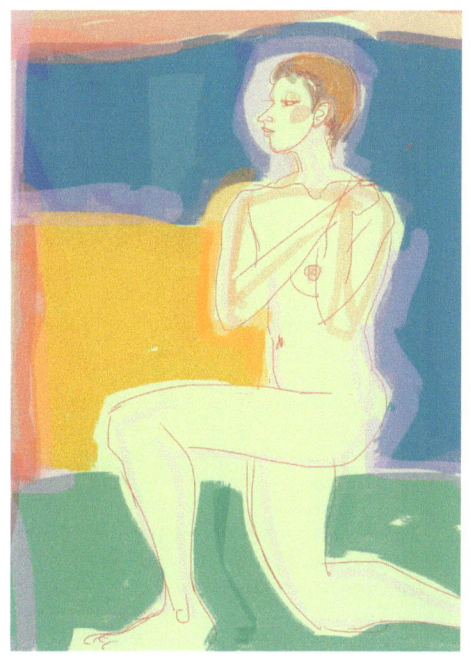

Susan R. Kirshenbaum

Gail Ragains

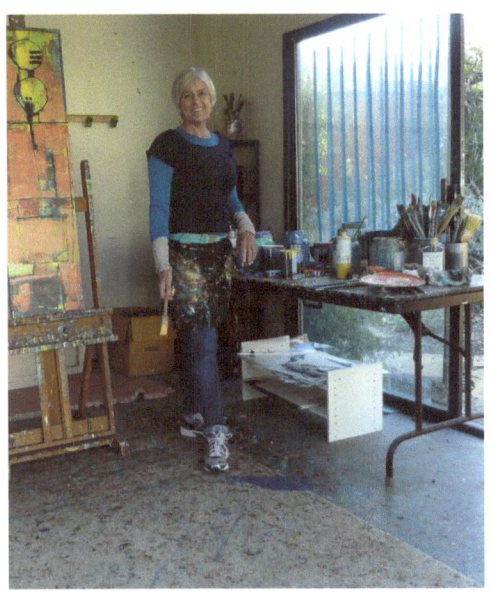

I approach each creative process as an open ended improvisation. Beginning with the structure of the figure or landscape I intuitively react to the paint, stripping away the non-essentials to give a loose interpretation of form, movement, and human expression. I look for the abstract shapes. I'm drawn to compelling colors, bold brushstrokes, and breaking rules.

I mainly work in acrylics and mixed media, but I always like to mix it up with new materials, and techniques to keep fresh. One thing that hasn't changed over the years is my ongoing discipline of drawing from live models.

website: http://www.gailragains.com
email: gailragains@comcast.net

GAIL RAGAINS was born, and raised in the San Francisco Bay Area. After a long time career as a Massage Therapist, she transitioned from massaging bodies, to painting and drawing them.

SELECT SOLO EXHIBITIONS:

2017	*Figurative Paintings*, Slate Contemporary- Hall Exhibition Oakland, CA
2013	*In the Moment*, Hang Art Gallery San Francisco, CA
2011	*California Figures*, Mountain View Center for the Performing Arts Mountain View, CA
2011	Kohler Jones Design Center, San Francisco, CA
2011	Canada College Main Theatre Gallery, Redwood City, CA
2011	Foster City Art Gallery, Foster City, CA
2010	Sequoia Hospital, Redwood City, CA
2008	Fremont Hills Country Club, Los Altos, CA
2007	The University Club, Palo Alto, CA

SELECT GROUP EXHIBITIONS:

2018	*Silhouettes*, San Ramon Valley Conference Center, San Ramon, CA (Slate Contemporary)
2017	*48 Pillars*, Arc Gallery, San Francisco, CA
	Figurative Painters, Spindrift Gallery, Gualala, CA
	Selected Works, Anne Nielson Fine Art, Charlotte North Carolina
	Celebrating Women Painters, Spindrift Gallery, Gualala, CA
2016	*Impulse*, Arc Gallery San Francisco, CA
	2016 Art Tour, Sea Ranch, CA
2015	*Hip to be Square*, Sopa Fine Arts, BC, Canada
	Summer Show, Ritz Carlton, Lake Tahoe , CA (Slate Contemporary)
	Salon At the Triton, Triton Museum, Santa Clara, CA
2014	*Wrapped in Color*, Sopa Fine Arts, BC, Canada
	Lines of Contradiction, Sopa Fine Arts, BC Canada
	Improper Nouns, Sopa Fine Arts, BC, Canada
	Anne and Mark's Art Party, Santa Clara County Fairground
2013	*Selected Works,* Jules Place, Boston, MA
	Off the Hook, Sopa Fine Arts, BC, Canada
	Under 8, Sopa Fine Arts, BC, Canada
2012	San Francisco Fine Art Fair, San Francisco, CA (represented by Hang Art)
	Same,Same, but Different, Hang Art Gallery, San Francisco, CA

PUBLICATIONS:

San Francisco Magazine May 22, 2012
Eight Local Artists to Watch: The Best of the Art Fairs, International Contemporary Artists Volume 12

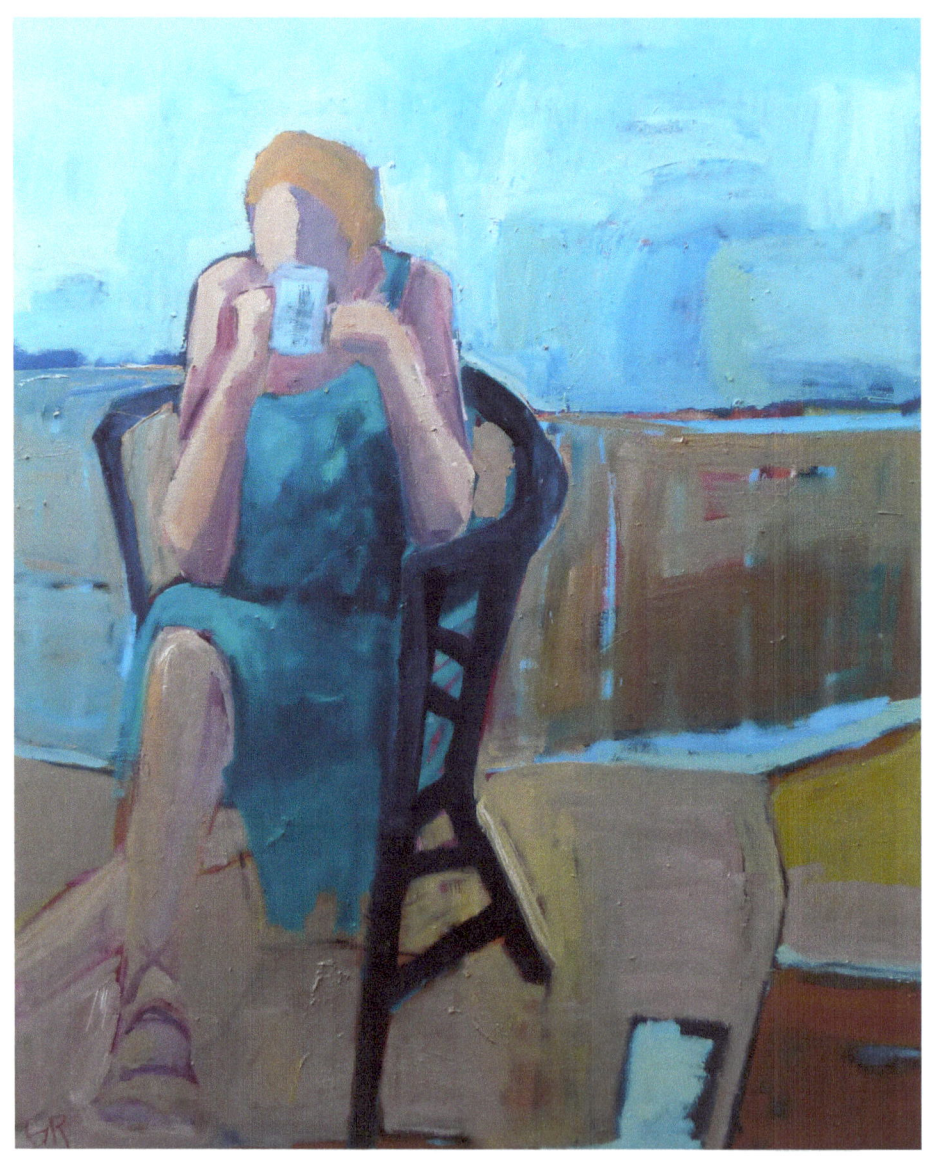

Woman Sipping Coffee
oil on canvas
48" x 60" $4700

Gail Ragains

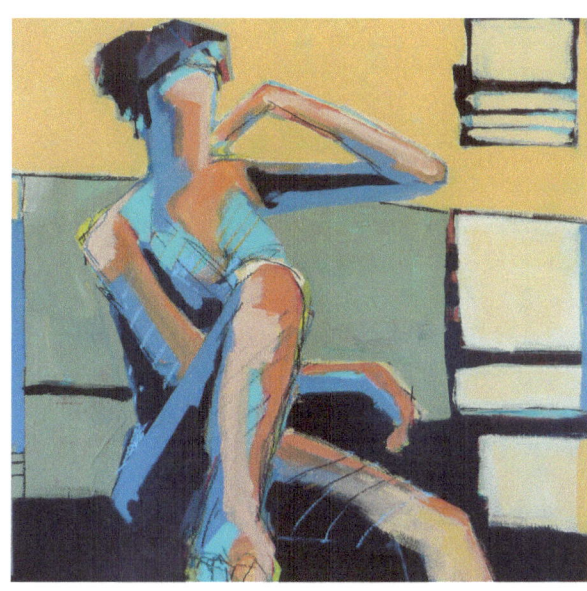

Afternoon Pose #1
acrylic on wood panel
24" x 24" $1125

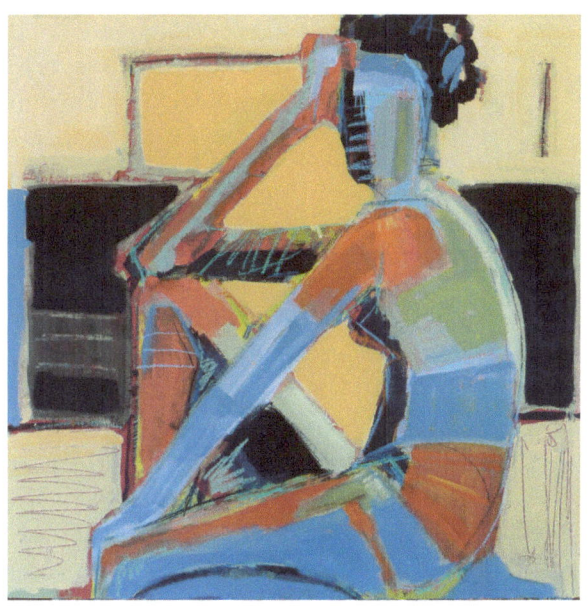

Afternoon Pose #2
acrylic on wood panel
24" x 24" $1125

Gail Ragains

Eric Saint Georges

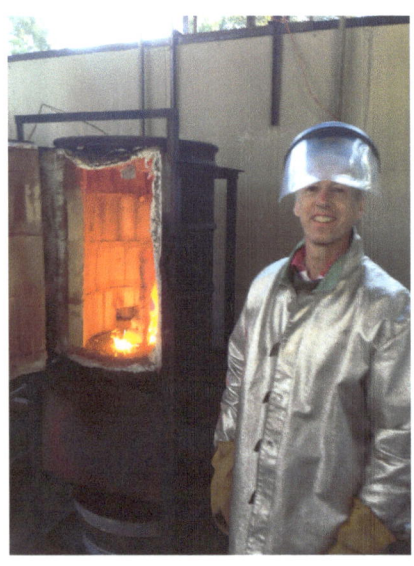

My current focus is on figurative sculpture and drawing. Even though I also enjoy carving once a while a stone or a beautiful piece of wood, my preferred sculpting medium is clay. In my drawings I like to combine charcoal, ink and watercolor. These mediums allow me to work quickly, my main interest being to capture life and energy in as spontaneous and raw a manner as possible.

I do most of my drawings from life models, my preference being very short poses. I like to draw very freely, with loose lines and watercolor strokes. I do not try to tell a story, as much as capturing the moment, the pose, the movement, the mood. I also do many of my sculptures from life as well.

I cast my sculptures in bronze, which is time consuming but very rewarding. I spend now my time between my studio in Los Gatos (CA), various life drawing sessions in the Bay area, and the West Valley College foundry.

website: http://www.ericsaintgeorges.com
email: contact@ericsaintgeorges.com

Born in Paris, France, ERIC SAINT GEORGES moved to the US in 1994.

As far as I can remember I have always been drawing and building things, but it is a workshop with the sculptor Petrus in 1978, which triggered my passion for sculpture. At that time, I had just completed my education in electrical engineering. Rather than going right away to work, I applied to the "Ecole Nationale Supérieure des Beaux Arts" in Paris, and studied drawing and sculpture there for 2 years, before spending several months with Petrus, from whom I learned the foundation of my clay technique. However, at the time, a career in art was not really an option for me (or so I thought) and I went back to pursuing a career as an engineer. Eventually, in 2015, after 35 years with limited artistic activity, I finally decided to go back to art full time.

SELECT EXHIBITIONS:

2017   Ruth Bancroft Sculpture Garden, Walnut Creek, CA (juried)
Statewide 2D Competition, Triton Museum of Art, Santa Clara CA (juried)
Gallery House, Palo Alto, CA
Form of a Woman, Neologian Gallery, San Mateo, CA (juried)
Vyne Bistro, San Jose, CA
Pacific Art League, Palo Alto CA (2nd Place)

2016   *Not so Heavy Metal II*, Mission College, San Jose CA (juried)
More the Merrier, Art Ark Gallery, San Jose CA (juried)
Instructor Exhibition, Pacific Art League, Palo Alto CA
California Clay Competition, The Artery, Davis CA
Figure and Faces, Pacific Art League, Palo Alto CA (juried)
Art Object Gallery, San Jose CA (celebrating International Sculpture Day)
Art Ark Gallery, San Jose CA (Silicon Valley Open Studio preview exhibition))
Pacific Art League, Palo Alto CA

2015   Main St Cafe, Los Altos, CA
Figure and Faces, Pacific Art League, Palo Alto CA (juried)

TEACHING:

2017 -   Instructor at Pacific Art League, Palo Alto CA (life drawing; figure sculpture)
Teaching Assistant, Metal Sculpture, West Valley College, CA

ART EDUCATION:

2015-16   Metal Sculpture at West Valley college (Saratoga) 2015-2016
1980-81   Resident with sculptor Petrus, France
1979-80   Ecole Nationale Supérieure des Beaux Arts, Paris, France. 1979-1980

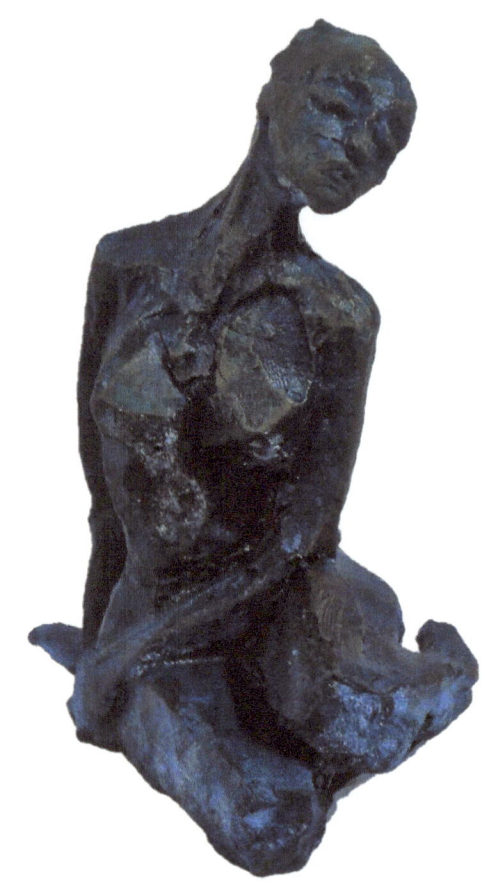

Rita
bronze
7" x 6" x 5" $900

Eric Saint Georges

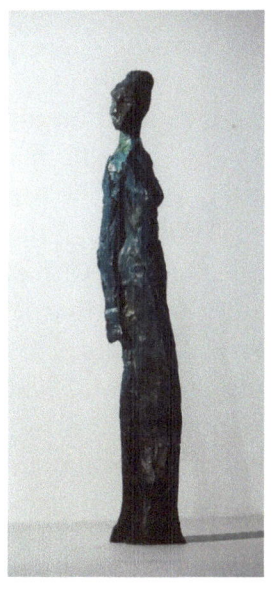

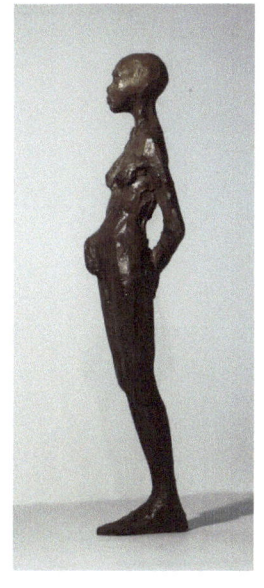

Elegant Bitch
bronze
14" x 3" x 3" $900

Anya
bronze
13" x 3" x 3" $900

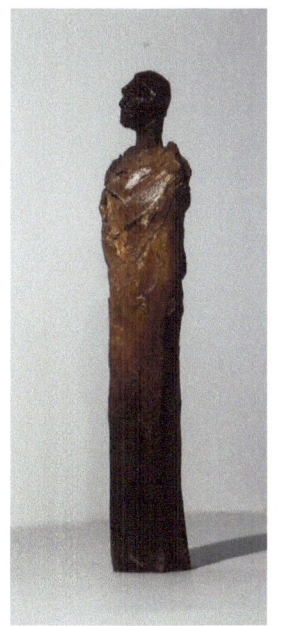

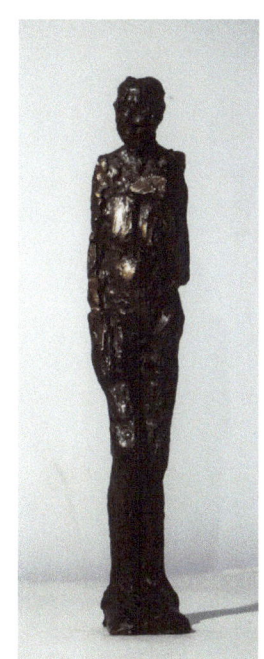

The Keeper
bronze
12" x 3" x 3" $900

Old Woman
bronze
13" x 3" x 3" $900

Eric Saint Georges

Julianne Wallace Sterling

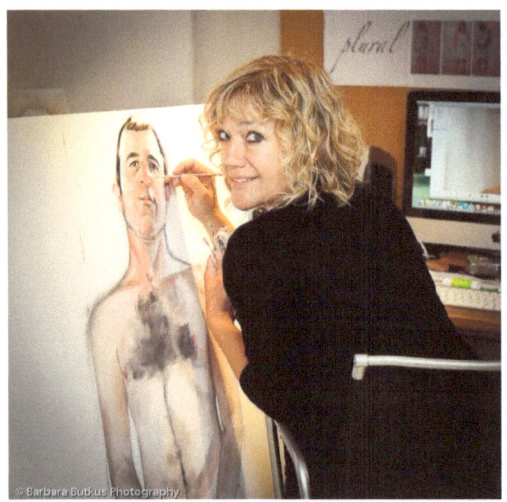

Julianne Wallace Sterling gives us figurative painting driven by the duality of paint made flesh and of flesh unmoored from practical gravity. The work reflects the rich history of portrait painting with figures that are exquisitely colored and drafted, yet with an underlying discomfort and strain. The artist also extends her themes into non-traditional media with nudes composed from Sharpie pen on styrofoam meat trays. Sterling's paintings explore the realities, complexities and absurdities of life as a woman, and this body of work illuminates the contingency and ambiguity of this social and cultural setting.

website: http://www.jsterlingart.com
email: juliannewsterling@gmail.com

EDUCATION:

1997-98 Cal State San Francisco, Studio Art, Post-Grad
1996-97 City College of San Francisco, Studio Art, Post-Grad
1993 University of California Riverside, BS Economics

RECENT SOLO EXHIBITIONS:

2017 *repose*, Mercury 20 Gallery, Oakland, CA
2016 *the digital camo*, Mercury 20 Gallery, Oakland, CA
2015 *unmoor*, Mercury 20 Gallery, Oakland, CA
2014 *for and against You*, Mercury 20 Gallery, Oakland, CA
2013 *plural*, Mercury 20 Gallery, Oakland, CA
2012 *this body*, Mercury 20 Gallery, Oakland, CA
2011 *Pushing Fairy Tales*, Mercury 20 Gallery, Oakland, CA
2010 *The Mommy Assassins*, Mercury 20 Gallery, Oakland, CA
Under Cover, Killing My Lobster, Zeum Theater at Yerba Buena, SF, CA

RECENT GROUP EXHIBITIONS:

2017 *EXISTE Y RESISTE*, Mission Cultural Center for Latino Arts, San Francisco, CA
2015 *The Opposite Sex*, online exhibition, Linus Gallery, Long Beach & Pasadena, CA
Voices: An Artist's Perspective, online exhibition Women's Caucus for Art, NAWA Gallery, NYC
Artists; Women, Vessel Gallery, Oakland, CA
Fusion, Arc Gallery, SAn Francisco CA
2013 *Tango and The Modern Nude*, Art Ark Gallery, San Jose, CA
2012 *The Nude 2012*, Studio Quercus, Oakland CA
2011 *Pro Arts Juried Annual 2011*, Oakland, CA
Premonition, Dacia Gallery, NY, NY
9th A.I.R. Gallery Biennial, Brooklyn, NY
2010 *Realism*, Artist-Xchange Gallery, SF, CA
Surface & Subtext, Mercury 20 Gallery, Oakland, CA
Speaking of Solitude, 6th National Juried Exhibition, Marin Museum of Contemporary Art, Novato, CA (first place)
Mercury Rising, Mercury 20 Gallery, Oakland, CA
Transformative Experience, Art@theOakbook, Oakland, CA

RECENT PRESS/PUBLICATIONS:

7x7.com, Culture, *Three Can't Miss Oakland Gallery Exhibits*, SF, October 2015
Unite Women, Voices an artist's perspective, NAWA Gallery, NY, NY June 2015
Fusion, Exhibition Catalog for Arc Gallery, SF May 2015
art ltd., Bay Area Supplement, May/June 2013
East Bay Express, *Staff Picks*, November 28, 2012
San Francisco Chronicle, *Critic's Pick*, June 14, 2012
East Bay Express, Arts & Culture, October, 19 2011
East Bay Express, Arts & Culture, June 15, 2011

PROFESSIONAL AFFILIATIONS:

Richmond Art Center, Richmond, CA;   Pro Arts, Oakland, CA;   Mercury Twenty Gallery, Oakland, CA

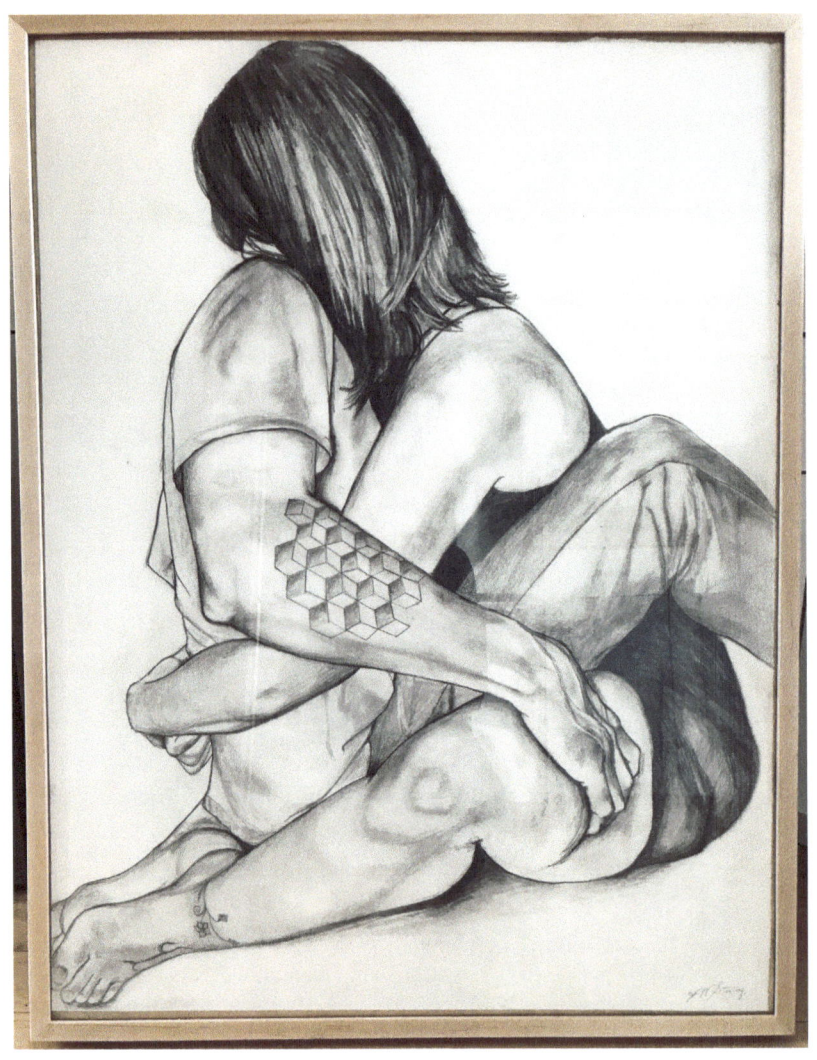

planets mixed up in you
graphite on BFK Rives
31" x 42" $1400

Julianne Wallace Sterling

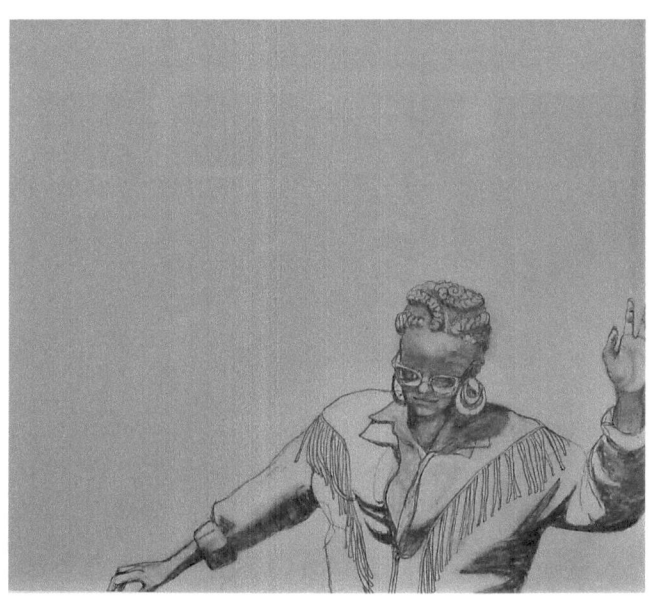

Fringe 1
graphite on acetate
16" x 13" $240

Fringe 2
graphite on acetate
13" x 16" $240

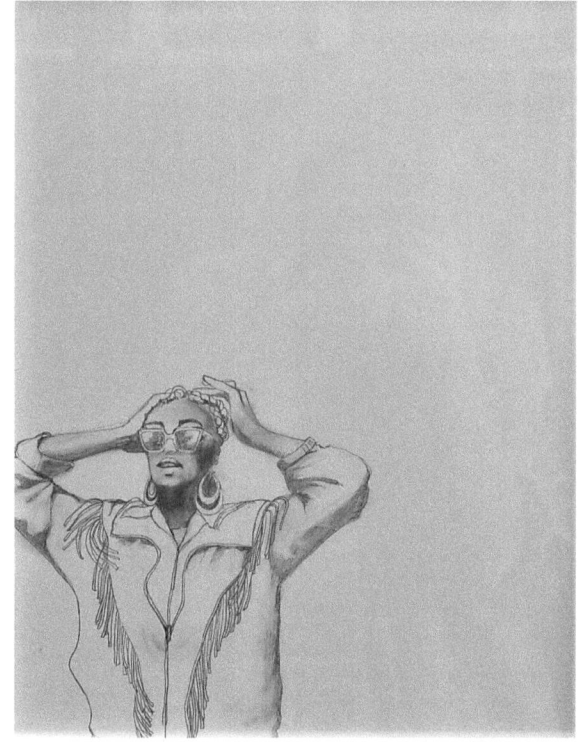

Julianne Wallace Sterling

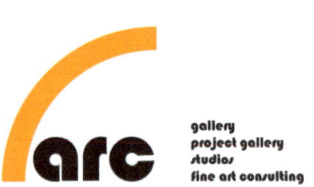

gallery
project gallery
studios
fine art consulting

1246 Folsom St.
San Francisco, CA

http://arc-sf.com
http://arcfinearts-sf.com
arcgallerysf@gmail.com
415-298-7969

www.ingramcontent.com/pod-product-compliance
Lightning Source LLC
Chambersburg PA
CBHW051835210526
45473CB00005B/1880